Quack! Quack! Quack!

Joyce Carol Kassin

Archway Publishing books may be ordered through booksellers or by contacting:

Archway Publishing
1663 Liberty Drive
Bloomington, IN 47403
www.archwaypublishing.com
844-669-3957

Interior Image Credit: Florence Husney

ISBN: 978-1-6657-1919-3 (sc)
ISBN: 978-1-6657-1920-9 (e)

Print information available on the last page.

Archway Publishing rev. date: 02/22/2022

ARCHWAY
PUBLISHING

Quack!

Quack!

Quack!

Once upon a time, there was a little old lady who lived on the second floor of an apartment building in Florida. It was her special place she went to during the winter months.

Her porch looked out to a waterway where boats come and go. Some boats were docked near the building. The lady enjoyed seeing all the different kinds of boats pass by.

There were small boats, taxi boats, motor boats, sail boats, and police boats that would check the waterways. It was very interesting and delightful.

One beautiful sunny morning, she opened the door to her large balcony and heard something. At first, it sounded like a squirrel.

When the lady went closer to the water, she saw a beautiful duck. He had a lovely coloring of blue, green, and brown feathers shining in the sunlight. He was quacking away.

It went like this:

quack quack quack quack quack-quack quack quack quack quack-quack quack quack.

The lady ran to get her camera and some bread.

She took his picture and then threw down the bread.

With barely a glance at the bread, the duck still kept complaining and quaking away like this:

quack quack quack quack quack- quack quack quack quack quack -quack quack quack.

A seagull swooped down and ate a piece of the bread.

The duck suddenly showed some interest in the food.
He took a piece of bread but he still was not happy.

So he started quaking again:
quack quack quack quack quack-quack quack quack quack.

The lady didn't know what to do for him, so she went into her apartment. In a few minutes, the quacking stopped.

The lady looked out the balcony again. What did she see? She saw that he was not quaking anymore. He was with a plain looking brown female duck. He was quacking because he wanted to be with his duck friend.

A few days later, the lady's vacation was almost over and she was about to go home to another city. Even though it was quiet out, she looked down from her balcony and guess what she saw. There was the beautiful duck with his plain looking lady duck friend.

The lady saw he was very happy to have his friend with him. Then the two ducks swam in the lovely waterways together, with him following after her. They swam happily ever after.

The end.

A true story.

Printed in the United States
by Baker & Taylor Publisher Services